GALE
CENGAGE Learning

Novels for Students, Volume 13

Staff

Editor: Elizabeth Thomason.

Contributing Editors: Anne Marie Hacht, Michael L. LaBlanc, Ira Mark Milne, Jennifer Smith, Carol Ullmann.

Managing Editor, Content: Dwayne D. Hayes.

Managing Editor, Product: David Galens.

Publisher, Literature Product: Mark Scott.

Literature Content Capture: Joyce Nakamura, *Managing Editor*. Sara Constantakis, *Editor*.

Research: Victoria B. Cariappa, *Research Manager*. Sarah Genik, Ron Morelli, Tamara Nott, Tracie A. Richardson, *Research Associates*. Nicodemus Ford, *Research Assistant*.

Permissions: Maria Franklin, *Permissions Manager*. Kim Davis, *Permissions Associate*.

Manufacturing: Mary Beth Trimper, *Manager, Composition and Electronic Prepress*. Evi Seoud, *Assistant Manager, Composition Purchasing and Electronic Prepress*. Stacy Melson, *Buyer*.

Imaging and Multimedia Content Team: Barbara Yarrow, *Manager*. Randy Bassett, *Imaging Supervisor*. Robert Duncan, Dan Newell, Luke Rademacher, *Imaging Specialists*. Pamela A. Reed, *Imaging Coordinator*. Leitha Etheridge-Sims, Mary Grimes, David G. Oblender, *Image Catalogers*. Robyn V. Young, *Project Manager*. Dean Dauphinais, *Senior Image Editor*. Kelly A. Quin, *Image Editor*.

Product Design Team: Pamela A. E. Galbreath, *Senior Art Director*. Michael Logusz, *Graphic Artist*.

Copyright Notice

of the publisher and verified to the satisfaction of the publisher will be corrected in future editions.

This publication is a creative work fully protected by all applicable copyright laws, as well as by misappropriation, trade secret, unfair competition, and other applicable laws. The authors and editors of this work have added value to the underlying factual material herein through one or more of the following: unique and original selection, coordination, expression, arrangement, and classification of the information. All rights to this publication will be vigorously defended.

The Optimist's Daughter

Eudora Welty

1972

Introduction

The first version of Eudora Welty's best-selling, Pulitzer Prize-winning novel, *The Optimist's Daughter*, appeared as a short story in 1969 in the *New Yorker*. Revised and published as a novel in 1972, it is considered by some to be her sparest novel. In fact, Welty herself thought of the novel as more akin to a short story than a true novel. The book's complexity arises not from its length but from the emotions of the characters.

The Optimist's Daughter is the story of Laurel,

a widow who returns to Mississippi when her father is ill and witnesses his death and funeral. From there, she embarks on a deeply personal journey to explore her past and her family in order to make sense of her future.

Welty's novel contains a number of autobiographical elements. Some of the male characters are inspired by Welty's uncles, and the women of the town represent Welty's observations on life in the South. Welty has stated that much of Becky McKelva's background is drawn from her mother's life in West Virginia. In fact, the novel was written not long after her mother's death, a period in which Welty was recalling her mother's life and experiences. In this way, the character of Laurel represents Welty's own desire to inquire into her past and understand how it affects her present and future.

Author Biography

Eudora Alice Welty was born in Jackson, Mississippi, on April 13, 1909, to Chestina and Christian Welty. With her two younger brothers, she was reared in Jackson, although neither of her parents was from the Deep South. Her father came from Ohio, and her mother was from West Virginia. Both were teachers by trade until the family moved to Mississippi, where Christian entered the insurance business.

Welty remembers a very happy childhood in which she was surrounded by books and loved listening to her parents read to each other in the evenings. She also remembers how much she loved listening to the ladies in town trade stories, and her habit of noting their speech patterns and colloquialisms served her well when she began writing about the South.

After completing her public education in Jackson, Welty attended Mississippi State College for Women from 1925 to 1927, finishing a bachelor of arts degree in 1929 at the University of Wisconsin. At the encouragement of her father (who wanted her to have a reliable trade), she studied advertising at Columbia University from 1930 to 1931.

When her father died suddenly, Welty returned home to settle in Jackson. She worked various jobs with newspapers and a radio station before going to work for the Works Progress Administration, a government program established during the Depression that assigned people to work on public projects for much-needed income. Welty also took up photography, snapping pictures of all kinds of people (mostly African Americans) in her native Mississippi.

Her first published story, "Death of a Traveling Salesman," appeared in 1936, after which Welty's stories were accepted by top publications such as *Atlantic* and *Southern Review*. During her early writing career, Welty's work was often narrowly defined as regionalist or feminist. Still, she was admired by other writers, and her first collection of short stories, *A Curtain of Green*, left critics eagerly anticipating Welty's future work. Over the next thirty years, Welty had over fifteen books published, including short fiction, novels, and non-fiction.

In the 1970s and 1980s, there was renewed interest in her work, partially because of the rise in feminist criticism. Although Welty prefers to distance herself from the efforts of feminists, the renewed interest demonstrated to a new generation of readers that her writing was much more than an easily categorized body of work. Readers and critics continue to be drawn to her writing for her subtle, unique style, her handling of daily life, and her depictions of everyday heroism.

Welty's work has been recognized with prestigious awards such as a Guggenheim Fellowship in 1942; the O. Henry Award in 1942,

1943, and 1968; the National Institute of Arts and Letters literary grant in 1944 and Gold Medal for fiction in 1972; and a Pulitzer Prize in 1973 for *The Optimist's Daughter*.

Welty died of pneumonia on July 23, 2001, in Jackson, Mississippi, at the age of 92.

Plot Summary

Part One

As *The Optimist's Daughter* opens, Laurel McKelva Hand leaves Chicago and goes to New Orleans, where her father, Judge McKelva, is seeing an eye specialist to find out why his sight is failing. Laurel meets her father's young, new wife, a selfish, disrespectful woman named Wanda Fay ("Fay"). The doctor tells Judge that he has a detached retina and that it must be operated on at once. After the operation, the eye seems to be recovering normally, but Judge's health is not bearing the rigors of surgery well. He is lethargic and his health declines. Laurel and Fay, along with another woman, watch Judge to assure that he does not move very much, which would jeopardize the recovery of his eye.

Laurel and Fay have adjoining rooms at a nearby hotel, but Laurel fails in her attempts to get to know Fay. Meanwhile, Judge is now sharing a hospital room with a man whose senility makes him speak and behave strangely. The man's loud, colorful family is always in the waiting room.

At one point, Fay decides to try to scare Judge back to vitality by shaking him, but he dies soon after this incident. Welty is never clear about whether or not Fay's action caused the death. The next day, Laurel and Fay board a train to Mount Salus, Mississippi, the McKelvas' hometown.

Part Two

Laurel and Fay arrive in Mount Salus, and Judge's coffin is taken off the train and loaded into a waiting hearse. Many of Laurel's old friends are waiting for her at the station. They go back to the house, where a few people are waiting. The next day, many neighbors and friends stop by the house to view Judge's body, to bring food for the family, and to socialize. Fay's family, the Chisoms, have been invited from Madrid, Texas, and their arrival creates quite a stir among the genteel southerners. The Chisoms are crude and loud and have no sense of decorum. When Fay finally emerges from her room, she screams and wails and throws herself on Judge's body before being dragged away. Next, the mourners go to the church for the funeral, where public turnout is impressive, and then they go to the cemetery for the burial.

When Laurel and Fay return home, there are a few lingering friends. Fay decides to return to Madrid with her family for a few days' visit and is happy to hear that Laurel will be gone in three days. Neither wants to run into the other, as they have found it impossible to get along.

Part Three

The next day, Laurel works in the garden while four elderly neighbor women sit and gossip about Fay. When Laurel goes inside, she walks through her father's library, taking in all the memories inspired by the books, furniture, and general clutter.

Later, she meets some friends to reminisce about the days before Laurel moved to Chicago. When she gets back to the house, Laurel finds that a bird has gotten inside. As she tries to trap it in a single room, she allows herself to think about how much she blames Fay for her father's death, which makes her long to be with her deceased mother.

Laurel goes into the sewing room, which was once her nursery. She finds her mother's small desk, filled with papers, photographs, and letters. A flood of memories washes over her, including the details of her mother's background in West Virginia, their relationship, and her mother's steady decline and death. Her sorrow leads her to remember her husband, Phil, who died in World War II. She imagines that they would have enjoyed the kind of happy marriage her parents had, if only his life had not been cut short.

Part Four

The next morning, with the help of Missouri (an African-American woman who has worked as a cook for the McKelvas since Laurel's childhood), Laurel manages to get the trapped bird out of the house. She packs her suitcase in preparation for her ride to the airport. When she goes into the kitchen, more memories come to her, and she finds her mother's breadboard that Phil had made for her. At the same time, Fay returns home and is irate that Laurel is still there. They argue about the breadboard and then about the importance of the past, and Laurel comes close to striking Fay with the breadboard. She stops herself and decides not to take the breadboard with her because she has come to understand that freedom is more powerful than memories. The knowledge she has gained about herself over the last few days has liberated her from the pain, despair, and sense of obligation she once felt.

Laurel hears her ride honk for her outside, and she hugs Missouri on her way out the door. As she rides out of town on her way to the airport, she waves back at the many people who are waving to her.

Characters

Mrs. Bolt

The minister's wife, Mrs. Bolt is an elderly neighbor woman. She is one of the local ladies who gossips about Fay.

Major Rupert Bullock

Major Bullock is a friend of Judge McKelva. After Judge's death, Major attends the wake and the funeral, making a big show of telling grand stories about his deceased friend. There is an indication that Major may have a drinking problem, although nothing more than a suggestion is made. Major differs from most of the neighbors in that he is sympathetic toward Fay. He embodies southern manners in his attitude toward Fay and when he escorts Laurel safely home in the rain.

Tennyson Bullock

Major Bullock's wife, Tennyson, is a neighbor and close friend of the McKelva family. Despite her husband's commanding presence, she seems to be the dominant one in their marriage. She is typical of the women in her community in that she enjoys sitting with the ladies, gossiping, or playing bridge. Mrs. Bullock is known for her subtle sarcasm.

Tish Bullock

Tish is an old friend of Laurel's. She is the daughter of Major and Tennyson Bullock. Tish was one of Laurel's bridesmaids and their friendship is still warm despite the fact that Laurel now lives in Chicago. Tish married the captain of the high school football team but is now divorced.

Bubba Chisom

Fay's brother, Bubba arrives at the wake inappropriately dressed in a windbreaker, insensitively complaining about how long a drive they took to get there, and grumbling about how they will have to turn around and do the whole drive again.

Grandpa Chisom

Grandpa Chisom is the only member of his family who seems to have any manners. He demonstrates his thoughtfulness by bringing Laurel a candy box full of pecans he has shelled for her. Unlike the rest of his family, he speaks kindly to her and tries to stay out of the way.

Mrs. Chisom

Mrs. Chisom is Fay's mother. She is insensitive and crude. Her only interest is in indulging her daughter, and she gives no thought to expressing any sympathy to anyone else in the house during the wake or the funeral. She is impressed with the money Fay now seems to have as Judge's widow. She suggests that the entire family should move into the house with Fay so she can turn it into a boarding house.

Sis Chisom

Fay's pregnant sister, Sis is no more refined or observant than her mother. She brings her young son to the funeral as a learning experience for him and proceeds to yell at him throughout the events of the day. She allows him to wear a cowboy outfit and say almost anything he pleases.

Adele Courtland

Dr. Courtland's sister, Adele is a nurturing woman who has known the McKelva family for many years and was Laurel's first-grade teacher. She is described as an elegant woman with an authoritative voice. She still wears her hair in the same bun that she wore back when Laurel was a child.

Dr. Nate Courtland

Dr. Courtland is the eye specialist Judge visits about his failing sight. Although Dr. Courtland practices in New Orleans, Judge makes the trip presumably because the two have been friends for so long. Their families know each other, and Judge even helped put his friend through medical school.

Media Adaptations

- Random House has produced two audio-book adaptations of *The Optimist's Daughter*, an unabridged version in 1986 and an abridged version in 1999. Both versions are read by Welty herself.

Mr. Dalzell

Mr. Dalzell shares a hospital room with Judge McKelva while he recovers from his eye surgery. Dalzell is senile, blind, mostly deaf, and speaks erratically. He is also from Mississippi and is convinced that Judge is his long-lost son, Archie Lee.

Fay

See Wanda Fay (Chisom) McKelva

Laurel McKelva Hand

Laurel is Judge McKelva's only child. Her mother named her after the state flower of West Virginia, her mother's home state. Laurel is in her mid-forties and is tall and slender with dark hair. She is a professional fabric designer in Chicago but flies to New Orleans, where her father is seeing a doctor. She then travels to Mississippi after her father's death, staying for the wake and the funeral. Laurel also spends a few days in her father's house (the house in which she was reared) in order to make peace with her past.

Among the many emotional challenges she faces is the acceptance of Fay, her father's new young wife, whom she blames for her father's death. Laurel and Fay fail to get along from the beginning, and it is heart-wrenching for Laurel to watch Fay take her mother's position in the house that is full of Laurel's childhood memories and cherished objects.

As a result of her personal struggles, Laurel begins evaluating her past and her parents' relationship, including her mother's death. Consequently, she also evaluates her own marriage and the untimely death of her husband, a naval officer named Philip Hand, in World War II. By the time she leaves to return to Chicago, she has made peace with her past and her present and is better equipped for her future.

Laurel is an intelligent and sensitive woman

who wants her parents to be remembered as they really were, not as larger-than-life figures. She is perhaps not assertive enough in her dealings with Fay, although there is a sense that Laurel never plans to see her again, anyway. Laurel is welcomed in Mount Salus as a native, having grown up there, but, having been away for so long, she is now able to see the people as they really are. For example, she overhears several neighborhood ladies gossiping about Fay, but refuses to participate. Still, she refrains from passing judgment on anyone in town because she loves them as family friends and past classmates.

Judge Clinton McKelva

Judge McKelva is a retired judge in the small town of Mount Salus, Mississippi. When the book opens, he is seventy-one years old, and is described as tall and heavy. He is a lifelong resident of the town and holds a prominent place in it. At one point, he was the mayor. He is respected by the entire community, from his legal associates to the African Americans in the town.

Judge is described as patient and fair. He enjoyed a long and happy marriage to his first wife, Becky, although he did not handle her declining health well. When she needed strength, he was filled with uncertainty and thus reacted by not reacting at all. Often, he chose denial, reasoning that everything would be all right because he loved her. Eventually, she died. Years later, he married a woman completely different from his first wife. Welty never offers an explanation as to why Judge married Fay, although the neighborhood ladies gossip about it.

Wanda Fay (Chisom) McKelva

Wanda Fay Chisom McKelva ("Fay") is Judge McKelva's second wife. She is small, thin, and blonde with blue eyes. They met at a Southern Bar Association conference, where Fay was a part-time employee in the typing pool. A month later, Judge brought her to his hometown and married her. She is significantly younger than he is (and a little younger than Laurel), and her crude ways prevent her from fitting in with the Mount Salus community.

Fay is selfish, rude, ignorant, and self-indulgent. When her husband is being seen by the eye specialist, she insists that his problem is nothing that nature will not heal on its own. When her husband is recovering from surgery, her attitude is one of being inconvenienced. Thinking she can scare her husband back to vitality, she shakes him and yells at him, shortly after which he dies. During the wake, she bursts from her room in black satin to create a scene. She is never shown expressing any genuine pain or grief.

After the funeral, Fay decides to return to Texas for a visit with her family. She has no understanding of how important the house is to Laurel, nor does she have any interest in sympathizing with her. She seems to entertain her mother's idea of turning the home into a boarding house. This demonstrates how little she understands the community or her husband's standing in it.

Missouri

Missouri is the African-American cook who has worked for the McKelvas since Laurel was a child. She is a matter-of-fact woman who is deeply sympathetic to Laurel's grief. She seems somewhat resentful of Fay.

Mrs. Pease

Mrs. Pease is an elderly neighbor woman. She is one of the ladies who gossips about Fay.

Themes

Making Peace with the Past

In *The Optimist's Daughter* Laurel is forced to make peace with her past and her present in order to go on with her future. The event of her father's death is difficult for her because she enjoyed a loving relationship with him, and even more so because his recent marriage to Fay, a selfish, impatient woman, forces Laurel to accept circumstances beyond her control. Having lost her mother, her husband, and now her father—all of whom she loved dearly—Laurel finds herself alone in the world and faced with the reality of giving up her childhood home to a woman she despises.

Fay returns home with her family for a short visit after the funeral, and Laurel's flight back to Chicago is not for three days. This leaves her with a few days alone in the house. She uses this time to reflect on the past and its joys and trials. Laurel recalls her mother's love of her own home in West Virginia and the difficult period of her extended illness leading to her death. Along with her mother's virtues, she remembers her mother's flaws, just as she does with her father. In the process, she makes peace with the fact that her parents were wonderful people, but only human, and she decides to preserve their memories honestly. Realizing that the truly substantial gifts her parents gave her are not objects in the house that can be willed to someone else, she is able to leave for Chicago in peace.

Topics for Further Study

- Consult psychology textbooks and journals on the subject of grief. From a psychological point of view, how would you evaluate Laurel's ways of handling her grief with reference to her mother, her husband, and her father? How would you evaluate Fay's manner of dealing with grief? Based on your knowledge of the characters' upbringings and backgrounds, why do you think these two women react so differently to the death of Judge McKelva?

- Identify an object (such as a piece of jewelry or furniture, a photo, a letter, or a medal) that makes you feel connected to your past or to someone in your family who has passed away. Take that object and a notebook to a quiet place where you can reflect on your feelings. Write down your feelings about this object and the people or experiences with which you associate it. Write in a stream-of-consciousness style so that you will have an of interior monologue on paper. Later, review what you have written and compare it to Welty's description of how Laurel felt about certain objects in the house in which she was reared.

- Different religions and cultures adopt different traditions and rituals for burying their dead. Learn more about the beliefs about death and the funeral practices in one religion, belief system, or culture which is different from your own (such as Judaism, Hinduism, Buddhism, Muhammadan, African religions, traditional Native-American customs or beliefs, Catholicism, Protestantism, etc.). Compare it to your own. What significant differences are there? What similarities are evident?

- With a partner, stage a debate in

which one of you argues that Judge McKelva was right to marry Fay, and the other argues that his marriage to Fay was a mistake. Each of you should support your argument with reasons and examples; point out weaknesses in your opponent's argument; and respond to your opponent's criticisms of your position.

Laurel confronts another painful chapter of her past as she revisits her memories of her marriage to Phil Hand, a naval officer killed in World War II. In her heart and mind, those years were blissful and full of promise; while she basks in the memories of their happiness, she must also feel the pain of everything left undone. The way she describes the image of Phil appearing to her suggests that she had kept his memory closed up tightly in a deep part of herself. Once she begins uncovering her past, however, she has no choice but to revisit this part of her past, too. In the end, she is able to finally make peace with the loss of her husband in her youth. By doing so, she leaves Mount Salus with a cleansed spirit, thus allowing her to bid farewell to the comfort of her hometown, because she is now comfortable within herself wherever she goes.

Family Relationships

Welty depicts a wide variety of family

relationships over the course of the novel. She shows several marriages in flashback, some healthy and vibrant and others confusing. Laurel and Phil's marriage seems to have been a healthy one that would have lasted, just as Judge and Becky's marriage thrived until Becky's death. Having grown up watching such a healthy relationship, it is little wonder that Laurel would make a similarly good choice for herself. Judge's marriage to Fay confounds everyone who knew and loved him, but it makes perfect sense to Fay's family. This incongruity is merely a matter of perspective; what Judge had to offer a woman was obvious to all, but what Fay had to offer a man was elusive to everybody except her family. Still, even one of the neighborhood gossips has to admit that if Judge was happy, it is nobody's place to judge.

Parent-child relationships are depicted through Laurel's childhood memories. She loved both of her parents and, as an only child, felt a deep sense of responsibility to them. Despite her mother's hurtful ranting after suffering a stroke, Laurel remained steadfast in her commitment to care for her. She excused her mother's behavior because she understood that it was not intentional, but also because her father's inability to deal with the situation left nobody else to be strong in such a difficult situation. When her father dies, Laurel objects when visitors to the house tell stories about him that, while well-meaning, are not true. She feels helpless to control the mayhem of the wake and the funeral, but remains committed to preserving an accurate memory of his life. She doesn't want stories told that make him larger than life or that attribute others' deeds to him. In the end, Laurel is only able to leave her hometown and her childhood home behind because she has examined honest memories of her parents and made peace with the decisions they made and the people they truly were.

Style

Contrast

Perhaps because *The Optimist's Daughter* is a short novel, Welty includes elements of contrast to create a sense of tension in the story. The plot is fairly straightforward, but its drama and depth come from the characters and the tense atmosphere that hangs over the events of the story until the end, when Laurel leaves for Chicago. That the tension lifts when it does signals to the reader that Laurel, the title character and center of the novel, has accomplished what she needed to accomplish on her unexpected trip home. It ensures the reader that resolution has been reached.

Welty's contrasts are both subtle and overt. Her description of the hospital hallway is an example of an overt contrast that hints at underlying tensions: "The whitened floor, the whitened walls and ceiling, were set with narrow bands of black receding into the distance." The title is a more subtle example, as the use of the word "optimist" is ironic. Judge McKelva called himself an optimist in jest, not because he was a pessimist but because he had little choice about circumstances like his detached retina: "He, who had been declared the optimist, had not once expressed hope. Now it was she [Laurel] who was offering it to him." Another example of contrast is when Laurel and Fay leave the hospital after

Judge McKelva's death and find themselves in the midst of a Mardi Gras celebration. Welty sets the solemn passing of a genteel man amid one of the largest, most raucous festivals in the United States, thus creating tension and contrast.

Symbolism

Welty's use of symbolism is typical of short story writers. Symbolism is an efficient use of words because it allows the writer to convey multiple messages in a single passage, exchange, or image. For example, Judge McKelva's ailment that takes him to the hospital is an eye condition. This suggests that his ability to see clearly is compromised by his age. This may be one reason why he chose to marry Fay, as Laurel suggests in her observation of Wendell, Sis Chisom's young son: "He was like a young, undriven, unfalsifying, unvindictive Fay. So Fay might have appeared, just at the beginning, to her aging father, with his slipping eyesight."

Laurel goes to close her father's casket so it can be taken to the cemetery for the funeral, but has difficulty with the weight of its lid. She is helped by Mr. Pitts, the undertaker, and her friend Tish, who "helped her to give up bearing the weight of that lid, to let it come down." Closing the lid to the casket is symbolic to Laurel, because it is her conscious choice to accept the end of her relationship with her father. It is literally the last time she will see him.

Perhaps the most dramatic example of

symbolism is when Laurel returns to her father's house alone to find that a bird has found its way inside. As she rushes to close interior doors to isolate the bird, she hears it flying against windows and doors, trying to escape. At the same time, she allows herself to form the thoughts that express that she blames Fay for her father's death. Her anger, resentment, and helplessness are struggling, along with the bird, to get out. As Laurel thinks about her case against Fay, Welty writes, "Why, it would stand up in court! Laurel thought, as she heard the bird beating against the door and felt the house itself shake in the rainy wind."

Omniscient Narrator

The narrator in *The Optimist's Daughter* is omniscient ("all-knowing"), meaning that the story is told from a third-person point-of-view. The narrator is not a character in the story, and is able to enter the thoughts of several different characters, but shows an obvious bias toward Laurel and other southern characters. The narrator is typical of an omniscient narrator in the telling of events, such as the wake at Judge McKelva's house, at which the narrator passes from room to room, describing the people and conversations along the way. The narrator also reveals the thoughts and feelings of several different characters, but never reveals those of Fay and her family. There are extended passages of Laurel's interior monologue, such as when she goes through her father's office, taking in the sight of every book, pile of papers, and piece of furniture.

As Laurel delves deeper into her heart, so does the narrator, as when Laurel finds her mother's old letters, papers, and photographs. While it is most often Laurel's thoughts that are revealed, the narrator also sees inside the minds of other residents of Mount Salus. For example, when Laurel insists that Major Bullock's story about her father frightening away the "White Caps" (members of the Ku Klux Klan) is not true, the narrator tells the reader that the Major's feelings were hurt.

Life in the South

The small town of Mount Salus represents the gentility and social life of the traditional South. Because of its commitment to tradition and its older population, Mount Salus reflects many of the values and beliefs of the Old South. Despite changes and progress, the people adhere to the chivalric, hierarchical social organization of the South. Family is extremely important, and a person's character is often attributed to his or her bloodline. People treat one another with outward respect and kindness, are quick to help their neighbors, and respect the older residents and natives of the town.

Fay is the subject of mean-spirited gossip, not only because she is an outsider, but also because she is crude and dramatic. In one scene, the older ladies in the neighborhood marvel that she does not know how to separate an egg, can only identify the frying pan in the kitchen, and does not cook Sunday dinner. To these ladies, one of whom is knitting an afghan, domestic skills are a fundamental part of femininity. That Fay's lack of familiarity with the kitchen is the cause of talk all over town is evidence of the narrowly defined roles that traditional southern people expect.

Religion in the South is almost exclusively Protestant, although there are Catholics and Jews.

While Baptists are most prominent, other denominations, such as United Methodist and Presbyterian, are also well-represented. Laurel's family, neighbors, and friends are all members of the Presbyterian Church, and they attribute many of Fay's unrefined ways to her being a Baptist.

Some historians believe that the endurance of southern manners and traditions is due to the hardships faced by the South in the past. Rather than tear it apart, they argue, the struggle to survive only made the culture stronger.

Southern Gothic Literature

Some of Welty's writing is associated with the southern gothic style, and there are elements of it in *The Optimist's Daughter*. This style features settings in the American South, fantastic incidents, and characters who are bizarre, grotesque, and outcast. Although the novels do not take place in drafty castles, mazes, and dark woods, the themes derived from such European gothic settings appear in southern gothic writing. These themes include isolation, confusion, and the search for meaning, all of which are reflected in the character of Laurel. Other characters in *The Optimist's Daughter* represent the bizarre, including Mr. Dalzell, whose senility causes him to act and speak strangely. Judge McKelva's funeral also offers examples of the bizarre and morbid, as when Miss Tennyson argues with Laurel over the viewing of her father's body. The presence at the funeral of Dot, Judge's secretary, is prompted not by grief but by the desire to take in the spectacle. Fay's erratic and disrespectful behavior is also grotesque.

Other writers associated with southern gothic writing include Tennessee Williams, Flannery O'Connor, Carson McCullers, William Faulkner, Katherine Anne Porter, and Truman Capote.

Critical Overview

Considered by many to be Welty's best novel, *The Optimist's Daughter* has garnered the admiration of readers and critics from the time of its publication to the present. In *U.S. News and World Report*, a critic declares that the publication of this novel secured Welty's position among the great American writers. Scholars find the novel so rich in material that many critical papers have been written about it, considering such ideas as Welty's use of landscape, her place among southern writers, and her portrayal of female characters, which many interpret as feminist in perspective.

Compare & Contrast

- **1970s:** After the death of a loved one, the family has the choice of having the body viewed at home or at the funeral parlor. It is not uncommon to have the viewing at home, in keeping with tradition.

  Today: People still have the option of having the body of a loved one viewed at home on the day of the funeral, although most families choose to have the viewing at the funeral parlor. There is variation according to ethnicity and religion.

- **1970s:** Racial tensions continue to discourage social interaction between African Americans and whites. While the law offers increased opportunities and rights to minorities, the culture is slow in catching up to this progress.

  Today: Racial tensions are still a part of everyday life, particularly in very large and very small cities. Strides have been impressive, however, and social interaction between races is both common and accepted.

- **1970s:** Traditional male and female roles are the norm. Women are primarily responsible for domestic duties, while men pursue careers to provide for their families. Opportunities exist for women, however, and the women's movement is bringing change.

  Today: Women are free to choose careers or to commit themselves exclusively to caring for their families, if their economic situations permit it. Women are entering the workforce in increasing numbers, and are even making their way into top leadership roles. At the same time, there is little if any stigma in choosing to be a full-time wife and mother.

Commentators are quick to praise Welty's stylistic choices in *The Optimist's Daughter*. Howard Moss of *New York Times Book Review* is impressed with Welty's skill in creating such a lush story in such a short novel. He describes it as "a miracle of compression, the kind of book, small in scope but profound in its implications, that rewards a lifetime of work." Detailing some of Welty's techniques, Welty scholar Ruth D. Weston writes in *Dictionary of Literary Biography*, "Welty's narrative virtuosity in *The Optimist's Daughter* provides continuing evidence of her modernist experimentation with the interior monologue and other narrative techniques, including character role reversals and split protagonists."

Welty's emphasis on the inner life as it relates to the outer world in this novel have led to comparisons with the acclaimed author Virginia Woolf. Moss notes that Welty's characteristic ability to write regional speech patterns is perfectly balanced with her attention to the truth about her characters. He explains, "Miss Welty is equally adept at redneck lingo, mountain twang and the evasions of middle-class speech, but it is in her inability to falsify feelings that gives the novel its particular sense of truth." Echoing this praise, the well-known literary critic Cleanth Brooks, in "Eudora Welty and the Southern Idiom," finds that this novel is one of Welty's "finest instances of her handling of the speech of the Southern folk."

Critics are often taken with Welty's ability to create unique and colorful characters who are completely realistic. Moss comments:

> there is a danger in *The Optimist's Daughter* of the case being stacked, of Laurel being too much the gentlewoman, and Fay too harshly the brash opportunist. In truth, Fay is a horror but eludes being evil.... Laurel is too nice but escapes being a prig.

Moss praises Welty's careful handling of these two opposing characters in such a way that neither is wholly good or wholly bad. Brooks expresses a similar sentiment when he comments,

> Wanda Fay is really awful ... and Wanda Fay's sister and mother are of the same stripe. But Miss Welty does not allow that even this family is wholly corrupted. Wanda Fay's grandfather, old Mr. Chisom, seems genuine enough, a decent old man.

A *Newsweek* review published at the time of the book's publication likens Welty's handling of her characters to that of Russian writer Anton Chekhov.

Many critics comment on the complex subject matter of the book. In *Twayne's United States Authors Series Online*, Ruth M. Vande Kieft observes:

Like no other work since a few of Eudora Welty's early stories, *The Optimist's Daughter* comes shrouded in what I have earlier called the dark or "sorrowful" mysteries of life and death, finally impenetrable. The weighting of terrible ambiguities and contraries in the novel has left many readers moved by its depth and beauty as by no other of Eudora Welty's works, and yet strangely baffled and saddened, as if the revelations heaped on Laurel, the understanding won by this intelligent, sensitive, truthful, and loving woman were not the final truth of the novel.

Edward Weeks of *Atlantic Monthly* is particularly drawn to Welty's use of "contrast," as mentioned by Vande Kieft in the above passage. Weeks praises Welty's portrayal of the contrast between the sentimental emotion of the neighbors and the insensitive, rude remarks made by the Chisoms during the funeral scenes. He finds that this contrast provides "shocking comedy" in that the reader is both amused and sympathetic. Commenting on the overt tension between Laurel and Fay, Moss writes, "Two kinds of people, two versions of life, two contending forces in America collide in *The Optimist's Daughter*. Its small dramatic battle sends reverberations in every direction."

That the novel continues to be read and analyzed by critics and scholars of all kinds is a testament to its depth and texture and to its lasting thematic and stylistic strengths.

Sources

Bailey, Beth, "Manners and Etiquette," in *Encyclopedia of American Social History*, Charles Scribner's Sons, 1993.

Brooks, Cleanth, "Eudora Welty and the Southern Idiom," in *Eudora Welty: A Form of Thanks*, edited by Louis Dollarhide and Ann J. Abadie, University Press of Mississippi, 1979, pp. 3-24.

Earle, Carville, "Rural Life in the South," in *Encyclopedia of American Social History*, Charles Scribner's Sons, 1993.

Moss, Howard, "Eudora Welty's New Novel about Death and Class," in *New York Times Book Review*, May 21, 1972.

Review of *The Optimist's Daughter, in Newsweek*, May 22, 1972.

Review of *The Optimist's Daughter*, in *U.S. News & World Report*, February 15, 1993.

Vande Kieft, Ruth M., "Eudora Welty," in *Concise Dictionary of American Literary Biography: The New Consciousness, 1941–1968*, Gale Research, 1987, pp. 492-505.

——————, "Eudora Welty," in *Twayne's United States Authors Series Online*, G. K. Hall & Co., 1999.

Weeks, Edward, Review of *The Optimist's Daughter*, in *Atlantic Monthly*, June 1972.

Weston, Ruth D., "Eudora Welty," in *Dictionary of Literary Biography*, Volume 143: *American Novelists Since World War II*, Gale Research, 1994, pp. 303-20.

Wolff, Sally, "Some Talk about Autobiography: An Interview with Eudora Welty," in *Southern Review*, Vol. 26, No. 1, January, 1990, pp. 81-88.

Further Reading

Bloom, Harold, *Eudora Welty: Comprehensive Research and Study Guide*, Chelsea House, 1999.

> Bloom offers a thorough reference to Welty's short stories, for which she is best known. Ideally suited for the reader new to Welty's work, this book explains themes, techniques, and contexts in Welty's short fiction.

Champion, Laurie, ed., *The Critical Response to Eudora Welty's Fiction*, Greenwood Publishing Group, 1994.

> This volume offers the collected criticism of Welty's writing from the 1940s to the present.

Price, Reynolds, ed., *Eudora Welty Photographs*, University Press of Mississippi, 1993.

> Using Welty's early photographs, Price depicts Welty's personal view of the South. The book includes an introductory interview with Welty, conducted by Price, concerning her photographs.

Weston, Ruth D., *Gothic Traditions and Narrative Techniques in the Fiction of Eudora Welty*, Louisiana State University Press, 1994.

> Weston reviews Welty's work in

terms of the gothic tradition to show how she uses gothic themes and narrative techniques within the southern literary framework.